Silent Echoes of Leadership

DEEPAK SHARMA

ISBN
paperback 979-8-89632-801-8
hardcase 979-8-89673-724-7

Disclaimer

The stories, characters, and scenarios presented in this book are fictional and are intended for illustrative purposes only. Any resemblance to actual persons, living or dead, or real-life events is purely coincidental. The situations, challenges, and experiences discussed are crafted to provide insight into leadership, personal growth, and self-awareness, and are not reflective of any specific individual, organization, or event.

While the lessons drawn throughout this book are based on real-world principles and observations, the characters and narratives are entirely imaginary and serve as a vehicle for the ideas explored in these pages. The intention is to offer inspiration and provoke thoughtful reflection, rather than to represent or mirror any particular real-life situation.

Readers are encouraged to apply the ideas and insights presented here in a way that is authentic to their own lives, understanding that the journey of leadership and personal development is unique to each individual.

Thank you for embarking on this journey with me—may these stories spark your own insights and guide you in your own leadership journey.

In silence, the seeds of wisdom grow,

Through storms unseen, where leaders go.

A whisper echoes, soft yet strong,

The silent scripts where we belong.

With every step, a question turns,

What is learned, and what still burns?

The unseen paths, the unknown calls,

Through rise, through falter—leadership falls.

Not answers sought, but courage found,

In the quiet moments, where truth is bound.

The heart of change, the soul of care,

In silent echoes, leaders dare.

–Deepak Sharma

Contents

Preface

"*Silent Echoes of Leadership*" is more than a book—it's a journey that invites you to explore the quiet but powerful qualities that make us not just leaders, but people of purpose, compassion, and resilience. As I write this, I reflect on the countless voices, experiences, and lessons that have guided me to this point. This book is my way of sharing the lessons learned, not from the loud applause of success but from the silent, introspective moments that define our paths.

In my role as a people leader, I have come to understand that true leadership is often born in silence: in the quiet moments of decision-making, in the unspoken challenges we face, and in the inner strength we cultivate. This book draws from those "silent scripts" of empathy, accountability, and cultural awareness—qualities that often go unnoticed but form the foundation of impactful leadership.

Throughout these pages, you will find insights and reflections on what it means to lead with heart and humility, to honour accountability as much as empathy, and to embrace change with an open mind. These are not just lessons for the boardroom or workplace; they are universal principles that speak to anyone seeking personal growth, self-responsibility, and a meaningful life.

My hope is that *Silent Echoes of Leadership* becomes a companion in your own journey—a reminder that leadership is a continuous process, shaped by our choices, our connections, and our commitment to being someone's someone. As you read, I encourage you to reflect, to question, and, most importantly, to see yourself not just as a follower of rules but as a leader in your own life, forging a path that is uniquely yours.

Thank you for taking this first step with me. Together, let us discover the quiet yet profound echoes that shape us, guide us, and lead us forward.

○ ○ ○

Acknowledgement

Writing *"Silent Echoes of Leadership"* has been a deeply personal and transformative experience, and it would not have been possible without the unwavering support of many individuals.

First, I would like to express my sincere gratitude to my family, whose love, encouragement, and belief in me have been the foundation on which this journey rests. To my closest friends, mentors, and colleagues—thank you for your honest feedback, inspiring conversations, and the countless hours you have spent listening to ideas that were, at times, just fragments of thought. Your presence in my life continues to shape who I am as both a person and a leader.

A special thanks to the many people I have had the privilege to work with throughout my career. Your experiences, challenges, and successes have influenced every page of this book. The silent, unspoken lessons I have learned from each of you have become the very essence of leadership that I now share.

I would also like to extend my heartfelt gratitude to the readers of this book. It is your curiosity, your thirst for knowledge, and your willingness to reflect and grow that inspired me to write this. I trust that this book will offer you not only insight and knowledge but also a deep sense of self-discovery.

Lastly, to those who have been the silent heroes in my life—the ones who lead with humility, empathy, and resilience, day in and day out, without fanfare or recognition—I dedicate this book to you. You are the true exemplars of leadership.

Chapter 1:

The Quiet Power of Inner Leadership

> **66** *Leadership begins where the noise ends, within the quiet depths of self-awareness.* **99**

I n a world that prizes external achievement, the idea of self-leadership can sometimes feel like an afterthought. But at its core, true leadership begins from within. When we learn to lead ourselves—to be responsible for our actions, our thoughts, and our growth—we set a foundation that supports everything else we do. Self-leadership is the quiet power that can transform not only individuals but also the teams, organizations, and communities around them.

Imagine a young manager, newly promoted and eager to make an impact. He's accustomed to external validation—a reassuring nod from his mentors, a word of praise after every achievement. But now, in this new role, he finds himself alone in decision-making moments, faced with challenges that test not just his skills but his values. This manager begins to realize that his success isn't measured by the approval of others but by his commitment to doing what's right, even when it goes unnoticed.

This journey is where self-responsibility begins.

The Courage to Own Our Choices

Self-leadership requires a willingness to face our own choices head-on. Often, it's easy to attribute success to skill and setbacks to circumstance. But leaders who take ownership of their actions, regardless of the outcome, experience a deeper growth. They begin to see each choice as an opportunity to align with their values. In the example of our young manager, he learns that true leadership doesn't come from his title but from his ability to own his decisions fully. He recognizes that self-responsibility is less about perfect choices and more about integrity and accountability.

Cultivating this inner leadership takes courage, as it requires us to confront uncomfortable truths about ourselves. In this journey, we begin to see that growth isn't always about moving forward. Sometimes, it's about pausing, reflecting, and adjusting our path. Self-responsibility is not just about accepting praise when things go right; it's also about owning mistakes with humility and using them as stepping stones.

One of the most challenging aspects of self-leadership is that its growth often goes unseen. Unlike external achievements, which are rewarded and acknowledged, inner growth is a quiet evolution. It doesn't come with applause or fanfare, yet it is the foundation on which all other successes are built.

Returning to our young manager, as he embraces self-responsibility, he notices that his team members start to respond differently. They trust him more, not because he always makes the right calls but because he's honest when he doesn't. His silent growth—though invisible to most—creates a ripple effect. His team begins to mirror his integrity, owning their actions and supporting each other in moments of struggle.

Self-leadership, therefore, is less about the visible markers of success and more about building resilience and authenticity from within. This journey teaches us that the greatest achievements in life are often those we achieve for ourselves.

A Quiet Invitation to Reflect

As you read these pages, I invite you to look inward. Think about the moments in your own life where you've led from within. Perhaps it was a decision you made because it aligned with your values, even when it was difficult. Or maybe it was a time when you held yourself accountable rather than looking for someone to share the blame. Self-leadership is something we all possess, and it is through these quiet acts of self-responsibility that we lay the groundwork for a life of purpose.

Have you ever found yourself acting from a place of fear rather than principle? Or making choices based on what others expect rather than what aligns with who you are? These are natural moments in anyone's journey, and they are often the starting points of deeper self-discovery. As we learn to listen to these silent prompts, we begin to find clarity in our actions and confidence in our direction.

Continuing the Journey

Self-responsibility and inner leadership are not destinations but lifelong companions. They grow with us, shaping our decisions, guiding our interactions, and defining our impact. This journey is one of constant learning—a commitment to lead ourselves before we seek to lead others. Our young manager's story doesn't end here; he continues to grow, learning each day that the quiet choices he makes, the values he upholds, and the responsibility he claims are what ultimately define him.

As you move forward through this book, consider this quiet power of inner leadership as your foundation.

It is where every chapter of growth, accountability, and impact begins. Whether you are a manager, an executive, or someone finding their way, the lessons of self-responsibility are universal, guiding us all in the silent, profound journey of becoming our best selves.

o o o

Chapter 2:

The Crossroad Within

"At times, life presents us with choices that aren't simply right or wrong but demand something deeper—a moment of truth where we must decide who we want to become."

Imagine standing at a juncture where no signboards exist, only whispers of possibility. You hesitate, knowing the step you take next will influence the story you're writing about your life. It's not just about the choice but about the quiet reckoning with oneself—an internal dialogue that questions, challenges, and sometimes unsettles.

Crossroads are universal. Whether it's deciding on a career change, committing to a personal relationship, or even smaller decisions that ripple over time, we all encounter these moments. But how often do we pause to ask ourselves if the direction we're choosing truly aligns with our inner compass?

For some, the weight of expectations—those imposed by society, family, or even our past selves—leads us down a path of "shoulds". The one where the approval of others becomes the silent navigator. For others, the pull of the unfamiliar may feel reckless, yet strangely compelling, like walking into fog trusting there's light on the other side.

Many of us feel the weight of uncertainty. The choices we make in these moments define our journey, shaping not just where we go but who we are. Often, the difficulty lies not in the options themselves but in the act of choosing—a process that demands clarity of values and the courage to act.

Imagine a young professional named Aarav. With a stable job, supportive colleagues, and predictable growth, he seemed set for a steady climb. But deep down, he felt stagnant—a quiet voice urged him toward something more meaningful. One day, an opportunity arose to lead a challenging project in a new city, far outside his comfort zone. It was a classic crossroad: the comfort of the known or the uncertainty of growth. Aarav hesitated but chose to embrace the unknown. While the path was difficult, it brought profound personal and professional transformation, revealing strengths he didn't know he had.

In moments like these, we often forget that the crossroads themselves are a gift. They force us to pause and reflect, to realign with what truly matters. Yet, the fear of failure, judgment, or regret can cloud our judgment, tempting us to remain in the safety of the familiar. But growth rarely thrives in the comfort zone—it emerges when we step into uncertainty with conviction.

To navigate such moments, one must cultivate inner awareness. This requires asking not just "What should I do?" but "Why does this matter to me?" The answers often reveal whether the choice aligns with your values or is merely driven by external expectations. When decisions stem from a deeper understanding of self, they bring clarity and direction, even in chaos.

While not every choice may yield immediate success, every step taken with intention builds resilience. Aarav's story is just one example, but we all have crossroads in our lives—some significant, others subtle. The courage to act transforms these moments into opportunities for growth.

As you stand at your own crossroads, take a moment to reflect: What does this choice say about who you are and who you aspire to become? The answer, though not always simple, often holds the key to your next step.

○ ○ ○

Chapter 3:

The Power of Perspective

"The way we choose to see the world shapes the world we experience."

Perspective is everything. It's the lens through which we perceive life, our surroundings, and the people we interact with. This lens defines not only how we react to challenges but also how we approach opportunities. Often, we find ourselves trapped in a narrow viewpoint, shaped by past experiences, fears, or external expectations. But true growth and transformation happen when we break free from these confines and shift our perspective.

Think about a time when a challenge seemed insurmountable—perhaps at work or in your personal life. Now, imagine if you could see that situation from a different angle, one where the challenge transforms into a lesson, an opportunity to build resilience or sharpen your skills. What would that shift in perspective feel like?

The world doesn't change based on our complaints or desires—it evolves through how we choose to engage with it. Our mindset shapes everything: the way we handle stress, the way we react to others, and even the way we define success.

The power of perspective lies in its ability to empower us. When we adopt a mindset of possibility instead of limitation, we begin to notice new opportunities. We find solutions rather than dwelling on problems. By changing our perspective, we gain control of how we respond to any situation. The power is ours.

But this shift requires intention. It's easy to fall back into old patterns, to react instinctively in a way that reinforces old beliefs and habits. The key is to practice awareness. When we become conscious of our thoughts and reactions, we can choose to shift them before they shape our reality.

Consider the impact of your perspective not only on your own journey but also on those around you. As a leader, as a colleague, or as a friend, your view of the world influences the way others perceive their own. When you approach challenges with optimism, curiosity, and a willingness to learn, you invite others to do the same. This ripple effect is powerful, creating a culture of growth and possibility.

Perspective isn't just about seeing things differently; it's about choosing to engage with life in a way that opens up new possibilities. It's a practice, one that requires effort and reflection. As you continue your journey, ask yourself: How might my perspective shift if I embraced challenges as opportunities for growth? What new doors could open if I reframe obstacles as stepping stones rather than roadblocks?

Your perspective has the power to transform your world. Embrace it.

ooo

Chapter 4:

The Value of Self-Reflection

"True wisdom begins with the courage to look within and understand oneself."

The moments of quiet often reveal what the noise conceals. In the rush to meet deadlines, fulfil commitments, and chase ambitions, there is little time to pause. Yet, it is in those pauses that clarity begins. Self-reflection doesn't demand elaborate rituals; it asks only for your attention.

Imagine a conversation—not with a friend, colleague, or mentor—but with yourself. A conversation free of judgment, focused instead on understanding. It starts with a simple question: *What have I learned about myself today?* The answers may not come immediately, and that's okay. Self-reflection is a practice, not a task to complete.

Think of a time when you made a choice, big or small, that didn't sit right with you afterward. Maybe it was an impulsive response or a decision that felt misaligned with your values. Did you take a moment to understand why it happened? Or did life move on, leaving that moment unexamined?

When you reflect, you do more than revisit your actions—you uncover the motivations behind them. Perhaps there was fear, a desire to please, or even misplaced confidence. These realizations don't weaken you; they strengthen you. They become lessons, shaping how you move forward.

Self-reflection is not a luxury reserved for quiet days; it's a discipline to carry into everyday life. It doesn't need hours of solitude—sometimes, a fleeting moment of thought during a commute or a quiet evening can be enough. It's about creating a habit of checking in with yourself, asking: *Am I moving closer to who I want to be, or further away?*

For many, the idea of self-reflection feels daunting. What if it uncovers uncomfortable truths? But these truths are not your enemy—they are guideposts. They reveal areas of growth and the strengths you may have overlooked. Without this inward gaze, it's easy to remain stuck in patterns that no longer serve you.

The value of self-reflection lies in its simplicity. It asks only for honesty and a willingness to see yourself as you are, not as you wish to appear. The mirror of reflection doesn't show perfection; it shows potential.

As you turn the page, consider taking a moment. Pause, breathe, and ask yourself: *What is one thing*

I've learned about myself this week? It may not feel significant now, but over time, these small moments of reflection can transform the way you understand and navigate life.

○ ○ ○

Chapter 5:

The Silent Shift: Discovering Inner Potential

"**True change often whispers before it roars.**"

Life has a way of nudging us, often silently, toward growth. Yet, these whispers are easy to miss in the noise of everyday demands. The silent shifts within us—the moments when we pause, reflect, and find clarity—are often the most transformative.

Imagine standing at a crossroads, not one that appears in front of you, but one within. This is where potential resides, waiting to be awakened. It doesn't shout or demand attention. It quietly asks, "Are you ready to listen?"

People often believe that growth comes only through grand gestures—promotions, accolades, or major life changes. But those who dig deeper realize that growth stems from an inner catalyst. It's the willingness to question, adapt, and embrace discomfort in pursuit of something greater.

Take Priya, for instance, a marketing executive known for her diligence. Despite her success, she felt a lingering void—a sense of untapped capability. Instead of ignoring it, she began to explore her discomfort. Small steps, like volunteering for unfamiliar projects and seeking feedback, created ripples that transformed her career. Priya's silent shift was her choice to evolve, even when the path wasn't clear.

Recognizing the Shift

Silent shifts often start with subtle signs—a feeling of dissatisfaction, a question you can't shake, or a realization that the current version of yourself no longer fits. Recognizing these signs requires mindfulness. Without awareness, these moments are easy to dismiss, leaving potential unexplored.

The key lies in trusting the process, even when the results aren't immediate. Growth is often invisible at first, like seeds sprouting beneath the soil. What matters is creating an environment where your potential can take root—by embracing curiosity, setting aside fear, and committing to continuous learning.

While it's easy to feel intimidated by the idea of personal transformation, the truth is that it begins with small, deliberate actions. Start by asking yourself:

> ➤ *What are the areas where I feel stuck or restless?*

> ➤ *What's one action I can take today to challenge myself?*

Remember, potential isn't unlocked in a single moment; it's revealed through consistent effort. The silent shift happens not when we wait for the right time but when we decide to create it.

By leaning into the subtle call of change, you not only discover your potential but also pave the way for others to do the same. Every silent shift, however small, creates a ripple effect that transforms not just individuals but the environments they touch.

○ ○ ○

Chapter 6:

The Practice of Self-Discipline

> **"**Self-discipline is not about control; it's about freedom—the freedom to create the life you envision.**"**

Self-discipline is a concept that many associate with restriction or rigid structure. However, in its truest form, self-discipline is about unlocking potential, not limiting it. It's the ability to make choices that serve your long-term goals, rather than yielding to short-term gratification. But it's not as simple as just saying "no" to temptations. It's about consciously choosing actions that align with your values and aspirations.

Consider the daily habits that shape your life. Every small action you take—whether it's exercising, managing time, or even the thoughts you nurture—requires discipline. And while it's easy to think of discipline in terms of following rules or setting boundaries, its true power lies in its ability to create sustainable results, not through force, but through choice.

Discipline is the cornerstone of personal mastery. It's not something that you either have or don't—it's something you build over time. Each decision you make, each moment of focus or restraint, is an opportunity to strengthen your ability to act in alignment with your deeper goals. It's a muscle that, like any other, requires consistent practice and intentional effort.

The first step is clarity. Without understanding what you truly want—your purpose, your values, your goals—discipline can feel like a burden, a list of obligations to fulfil. When you are clear on what matters most, self-discipline becomes a tool for achieving those desires. It is no longer something you must do, but something you get to do.

Think of discipline as a bridge between your present self and the person you want to become. It allows you to prioritize what's important over what's easy. It's easy to hit the snooze button, to delay hard tasks, or to give in to distractions. But discipline teaches us to do what's necessary even when it's difficult, to make decisions today that your future self will thank you for.

Self-discipline also involves understanding the power of habits. Habits are the small actions, repeated consistently, that shape our daily lives. A single act of discipline may not feel monumental, but compounded over time, it leads to profound change. Small adjustments in behaviour can add up to significant shifts in your mindset, productivity, and overall success.

Moreover, self-discipline is not about perfection; it's about consistency. The most successful individuals aren't necessarily the most talented or gifted—they are the ones who commit to doing the work, even on days when motivation is low. They make decisions with their future in mind, not their immediate desires.

One of the greatest challenges to self-discipline is distraction. The world around us is filled with opportunities to divert our attention—social media, email notifications, and other people's agendas. Self-discipline requires that we learn to manage these distractions and stay focused on what truly matters.

Remember, discipline is not a punishment. It's a tool that gives you the power to focus your energy where it matters. The more disciplined you become, the more you find that you have the freedom to pursue your highest goals. By exercising restraint in small, daily choices, you create the space and the energy to accomplish great things.

So, ask yourself: What areas of your life could benefit from more self-discipline? Where are you letting distractions or instant gratification take precedence over your long-term goals? Self-discipline isn't about being perfect—it's about taking one step after another with intention and purpose.

Start small. Choose one area of your life where you can build discipline. Whether it's sticking to a workout plan, prioritizing your most important work, or setting boundaries with your time, each step you take strengthens your ability to stay focused on the bigger picture.

Self-discipline is not about control; it's about the freedom to make your dreams a reality. With each act of discipline, you get closer to the person you want to become.

o o o

Chapter 7:

Leading with Empathy

"Empathy is the engine of a thriving workplace, where humanity and progress walk hand in hand."

Empathy often feels like a quiet force in leadership—steady, unassuming, and immensely powerful. It doesn't demand attention but earns respect through understanding, compassion, and connection. In the intricate dance of leadership, empathy serves as both the anchor and the wind, grounding leaders in humanity while propelling teams toward success.

Empathy is more than understanding someone else's perspective. It's the ability to step into their reality, even when it differs from your own. It's not about fixing every problem but about truly seeing the individual behind the role and recognizing their struggles, aspirations, and humanity.

A Subtle Yet Transformative Force

Consider this: a leader who actively listens without interruption, who notices the unsaid emotions in a meeting, or who takes time to understand a struggling team member's challenges. These seemingly small acts create a ripple effect. They foster trust, ignite loyalty, and cultivate a culture where people feel valued beyond their contributions.

Empathy thrives in the quiet moments of leadership: a simple pause in a conversation to reflect, an unexpected act of kindness, or a decision made with people in mind rather than just the bottom line. It's not about perfection but intention—a consistent effort to understand, connect, and support.

Why Empathy Matters

Workplaces often demand results, and leaders face immense pressure to deliver. But empathy is not a distraction from results; it's an enabler of them. Empathy creates space for innovation, collaboration, and resilience. It allows leaders to inspire rather than coerce, building teams that perform not out of obligation but out of shared purpose and belonging.

A workplace without empathy risks becoming transactional. In contrast, empathy transforms workplaces into communities where every individual feels seen and heard. This isn't just an idealistic vision—it's a measurable advantage. Studies show that empathetic leadership correlates with higher engagement, lower attrition, and a stronger sense of commitment across teams.

To lead with empathy is to embrace the complexity of human emotions while staying true to your purpose as a leader. It means asking yourself, in every interaction: *"Have I truly listened? Have I truly understood?"* Empathy may not always lead to easy answers, but it will guide you toward thoughtful actions.

As you step forward in your leadership journey, remember empathy is not a destination but a practice. It evolves with every conversation, every challenge, and every moment you choose to lead with humanity. In doing so, you not only uplift those around you but also discover a deeper, more fulfilling sense of leadership within yourself.

o o o

Chapter 8:

The Power of Self-Responsibility

❝Taking responsibility for your actions is not just about ownership, it's about unlocking your potential and creating the future you want to see.❞

Self-responsibility is often seen as an individual's duty to take ownership of their actions, decisions, and outcomes. But beyond this surface-level understanding, self-responsibility holds the power to shape not only personal success but also the success of the organizations we contribute to. It is the driving force that transforms passive compliance into active engagement, ensuring that every individual has the ability to shape their journey.

When we embrace self-responsibility, we acknowledge that we are the architects of our fate. It's easy to point to external circumstances—the economy, the job market, the actions of others—as reasons for setbacks or disappointments. But the reality is, we always have the power to decide how we respond to any situation. The most successful individuals don't allow circumstances to define them; instead, they use their ability to choose how to react as a lever to propel themselves forward.

At its core, self-responsibility is about recognizing that you are in charge of your outcomes. Whether it's your career, your relationships, or your personal growth, you are responsible for your actions, choices, and reactions. No one else can do this for you. By taking ownership, you empower yourself to take purposeful steps toward your goals and to ensure that you are always in alignment with your values.

Self-responsibility is deeply connected to the idea of personal integrity. It's about doing what you say you will do, even when no one is watching. It's about standing by your decisions, owning your mistakes, and being willing to learn and grow from them. People who practice self-responsibility are those who are accountable not only to others but, more importantly, to themselves. They know that true growth comes from taking responsibility for their actions, learning from them, and moving forward with a clear sense of purpose.

In the workplace, self-responsibility doesn't just benefit individuals—it drives the success of teams and organizations. When everyone in an organization takes responsibility for their work, there's no need for constant supervision or micromanagement. Each person becomes an integral part of the whole, driving success from within.

Moreover, when self-responsibility is ingrained in the culture of an organization, it fosters a sense of ownership and pride. Employees are more likely to take initiative, go above and beyond, and make decisions that benefit the organization as a whole. This culture creates an environment where individuals feel empowered to take risks, innovate, and pursue excellence because they know that they are directly accountable for the outcomes.

This culture of responsibility doesn't just improve productivity; it also enhances relationships. When people hold themselves accountable for their actions, they build trust within teams. Trust is the foundation of any strong organization, and it can only be achieved when individuals take responsibility for their roles and commitments.

To practice self-responsibility effectively, it's important to start with a mindset shift. Instead of seeing challenges or mistakes as setbacks, see them as opportunities to grow and improve. Self-responsibility isn't about always being perfect; it's about taking ownership, learning from your experiences, and striving to do better each day.

There is also power in acknowledging your achievements. While self-responsibility often focuses on owning your mistakes, it's equally important to recognize and celebrate the successes you create through your effort. This builds confidence and reinforces the behaviours that led to success in the first place.

Self-responsibility requires a clear vision of what you want to achieve and the discipline to take consistent steps toward that vision. It's about making deliberate choices every day, rather than leaving your future to chance. Whether it's through investing time in learning, improving relationships, or pursuing goals, the ability to take responsibility for your actions creates a roadmap to success.

Ultimately, self-responsibility is about creating your own legacy. You are the author of your story, and only you have the power to write your narrative. The choices you make today will define who you become tomorrow. The more you take responsibility for your actions, the more you will realize your potential and achieve the success you've always wanted.

> *So, as you move forward in your journey, ask yourself: What areas of your life could benefit from a greater sense of self-responsibility? Are you truly owning your decisions and their consequences? Are you actively shaping your path, or waiting for external circumstances to dictate your future?*

Embrace the power of self-responsibility, not just as a personal value, but as the catalyst that will drive your success, enhance your relationships, and elevate your career.

o o o

Chapter 9:

Finding Clarity: Owning Your Path

66 *Clarity isn't just about knowing where you're headed; it's about understanding why you're going there and how you'll get there.* **99**

Finding clarity is the foundation of all meaningful progress. It's the compass that guides you when faced with decisions, challenges, and opportunities. Without clarity, we often drift aimlessly, overwhelmed by distractions and lost in the noise of life. When we gain clarity, however, everything shifts. We become intentional in our choices, deliberate in our actions, and focused on our purpose. The fog of uncertainty lifts, and the path forward becomes clear.

But clarity isn't something that simply happens by chance. It requires introspection, alignment, and purpose. It's about understanding not just where you want to go, but why you want to go there. Without a strong sense of purpose, clarity is fleeting. When your purpose is clear, however, every decision you make, every step you take, becomes an extension of that purpose, propelling you forward with confidence.

To gain clarity, start by taking a step back and reflecting on your life—your values, your goals, your aspirations. What truly matters to you? What are the things that energise you, that make you feel alive? Once you understand what drives you, you can begin to align your actions with these deeper motivations.

When your actions are aligned with your purpose, you experience a sense of direction and fulfilment that is impossible to find elsewhere.

Clarity also requires setting boundaries—defining what is important and what is not. It's easy to get caught up in the demands of others or the distractions of the world around us. But without clarity, we can easily fall into the trap of reacting to external circumstances instead of proactively choosing our path. By setting clear boundaries around what matters, we create the mental space necessary for focused action and purposeful living.

This is where ownership comes in. To truly own your path, you must take full responsibility for where you are and where you want to go. It's not about blaming others or waiting for the right opportunity. It's about actively creating your future by making intentional decisions that align with your values and goals. When you take ownership of your path, you empower yourself to take control of your future.

One of the most powerful tools for gaining clarity is learning to trust yourself. Too often, we second-guess our decisions or let the opinions of others drown out our own intuition. The truth is, no one knows you better than you know yourself. Trusting your instincts and following your internal compass gives you the confidence to move forward, even when the path is unclear.

Moreover, clarity requires consistency. It's not enough to have a moment of insight; you must continuously reaffirm your commitment to your goals and purpose. Each day, you need to remind yourself why you are on this journey and what you hope to achieve. This consistency helps you stay grounded, even when obstacles arise. It also ensures that every action you take is aligned with your overarching vision.

It's also important to recognize that clarity doesn't always come in a straight line. Life is unpredictable, and the path to success is rarely a smooth one. At times, clarity may seem elusive, and the road ahead may feel uncertain. However, it's in these moments of discomfort that growth happens. Sometimes, the process of searching for clarity leads us to deeper insights about ourselves and the world around us. It's in these moments of uncertainty that we refine our vision and align ourselves even more closely with our true purpose.

Finding clarity doesn't mean having all the answers; it means knowing where to focus your energy and attention. It's about understanding what is most important to you and how to align your decisions with that vision. It's about living intentionally and with purpose, rather than simply reacting to the demands of life.

When you gain clarity, you stop living on autopilot. Instead, you begin to live consciously, making each decision with purpose and awareness. You start to see the connections between your actions and your outcomes. You understand that every choice you make is shaping your future, and you own that process completely.

As you begin to own your path, remember that clarity is not a one-time event—it's an ongoing journey. It evolves with you as you grow, learn, and experience life. What is clear to you today may shift as you gain new perspectives or develop new insights. Embrace this fluidity, knowing that the more you align yourself with your values, the more clarity will emerge.

Ultimately, the power of clarity lies in its ability to create momentum. When you are clear about your purpose, everything else falls into place.

Your goals become more achievable, your actions more effective, and your mindset more resilient. Clarity fuels your drive, giving you the strength and determination to continue moving forward, no matter the obstacles you encounter.

So, as you reflect on your journey, ask yourself: Where do I need more clarity in my life? What steps can I take to align my actions with my deepest values? How can I own my path more fully, knowing that each decision is shaping the future I want to create?

By embracing clarity and taking full ownership of your path, you unlock the power to live a life that is true to who you are and the goals you've set for yourself. And in doing so, you create the future you've always envisioned.

o o o

Chapter 10:

Embracing the Unwritten: Courage to Refine Success

There's a concept in life that often gets overlooked in our pursuit of success: the unwritten. Success, as it is often defined, can feel rigid, predefined, and bound by rules and outcomes. But true growth and achievement come when we allow ourselves the courage to embrace the unknown and the unwritten. Success is not solely about reaching a set goal—it's about how we evolve along the way and how we respond to the challenges and opportunities that arise when the road is not clearly marked.

We all have a vision of success, a set of milestones we believe will define our achievement. However, the real beauty of success lies in its unpredictability. It's the space between the lines, the opportunities that weren't anticipated, and the lessons that come from the unknown that make the journey worthwhile. To truly embrace success, we need to move beyond the conventional and be willing to step into areas that are not mapped out for us.

This requires courage. The courage to fail, the courage to pivot, and the courage to redefine our vision of success. The unwritten path is filled with ambiguity, but it also holds the potential for true transformation. When we only follow the path laid out by others or by our own preconceived notions, we miss out on the deeper, more meaningful opportunities that life has to offer.

Refining success means giving up the need for certainty and embracing the fluidity of the journey. It means recognizing that success isn't a fixed point in time but a dynamic, ever-changing experience. The person you are today is different from the person you will be tomorrow, and your version of success will continue to evolve as you grow. Success is a reflection of your journey, not just a destination.

Embracing the unwritten allows us to redefine success on our own terms. It's not about blindly following societal expectations or living up to someone else's definition of what success looks like. It's about discovering what success means for you. Perhaps it's in the relationships you build, the impact you have on others, or the fulfilment you find in everyday moments. By embracing the unwritten, you free yourself from external pressures and create your own unique version of success.

The beauty of the unwritten lies in the space it offers for exploration. When you let go of the need for rigid goals and timelines, you allow yourself the freedom to explore new ideas, new ways of thinking, and new ways of being. You open yourself to possibilities that would have otherwise remained closed, simply because you were too focused on following a script that had already been written.

Success that is solely defined by external standards can feel shallow and unsatisfying. But when you begin to define your own success, you tap into something deeper. You understand that success is not just about what you achieve, but how you feel about the journey along the way. It's about the impact you make, the growth you experience, and the ways in which you evolve as a person.

As you move forward, it's important to stay connected to this deeper sense of success. Ask yourself: What does success mean to me now? How has my understanding of success shifted as I have grown? And perhaps most importantly, how can I continue to redefine success in a way that honours my values, my aspirations, and my unique journey?

Embracing the unwritten is about having the courage to trust yourself and the process. It's about knowing that even when things don't go according to plan, you're still on the right path. It's about finding joy in the unknown and trusting that the experiences, challenges, and opportunities that arise will contribute to your growth.

Success is not just about achieving predefined goals—it's about embracing the fullness of life, with all its uncertainties and possibilities. It's about having the courage to make decisions that may not always make sense to others but feel right to you. The unwritten chapters are often the most powerful ones because they are where true transformation happens.

To refine your understanding of success, you must be willing to embrace the unwritten. Let go of the need for complete control and certainty, and instead, lean into the unknown. Trust that the path you are creating is the one meant for you. And when you look back on your journey, you'll see that the moments of growth, the ones that shaped your true success, were the ones you could never have predicted.

ooo

Chapter 11:

The Quiet Influence of Authentic Leadership

“*True leadership doesn't seek attention; it creates impact through consistency, humility, and trust.***”**

Authentic leadership is a quiet force. It's not about loud proclamations or commanding attention in every room. Instead, authentic leadership is about being genuine, transparent, and true to oneself, even when no one is watching. It's the subtle but profound influence that comes from being consistent in your values, showing vulnerability when necessary, and leading by example.

Many people mistakenly believe that leadership is about power, control, or dominance. But the most effective leaders are those who inspire, support, and empower others. Authentic leaders don't need to impress others with their titles or accomplishments. Their true influence is in the way they make people feel—empowered, valued, and heard.

In today's fast-paced and often chaotic world, leadership can sometimes be distorted by the pressures of external expectations or the constant pursuit of success. But authentic leadership doesn't conform to these pressures. Instead, it's rooted in self-awareness and a deep commitment to staying true to one's principles, no matter the external circumstances.

The quiet influence of authentic leadership comes from the ability to build trust—trust with colleagues, teams, and peers. Trust is the foundation of any strong relationship, and leadership is no exception. When leaders show up consistently, acting with integrity and honesty, they create an environment where people feel safe, respected, and motivated. Authentic leaders build trust not by forcing it but by earning it every day, through their actions and decisions.

The true measure of a leader's influence lies in the impact they have on others. It's about how they nurture the growth of individuals within their teams, how they support others in overcoming challenges, and how they create an environment where people feel empowered to contribute their best selves. Authentic leaders understand that leadership is not a position of power but a responsibility to uplift and guide others.

One of the key qualities of authentic leadership is vulnerability. It's not about having all the answers or pretending to be invincible. Instead, authentic leaders embrace vulnerability by admitting when they don't know something, asking for help when needed, and being open to feedback and growth. This openness builds trust and creates an environment where others feel comfortable doing the same.

Authentic leadership also involves emotional intelligence—the ability to understand, manage, and express one's emotions, as well as to empathise with the emotions of others. Emotional intelligence allows leaders to connect with people on a deeper level, to listen attentively, and to understand the nuances of their needs and concerns. This emotional awareness helps leaders to build stronger relationships and to navigate difficult situations with compassion and understanding.

At its core, authentic leadership is about leading with purpose. It's about being driven by a sense of meaning that transcends personal gain or external recognition. Authentic leaders are aligned with their values, and their decisions and actions are guided by a deeper sense of responsibility. They are not motivated by the desire for fame or accolades but by the desire to make a positive impact on the lives of others.

Authentic leadership is not always easy. It requires courage, especially when faced with adversity or situations that challenge one's values. It takes strength to lead authentically in environments that may not prioritize authenticity, and it takes resilience to stay true to oneself when it seems easier to conform. But the reward of leading authentically is immeasurable. The impact on the people you lead, the sense of fulfilment in knowing you've stayed true to your values, and the legacy you create are all worth the effort.

In the end, the quiet influence of authentic leadership is its power. It's the kind of leadership that doesn't need to be loud or boastful. It's the kind that quietly shifts the culture of an organization, the kind that leaves a lasting legacy. Authentic leaders create positive change not through force but through genuine connection, trust, and influence.

When you lead authentically, you create a ripple effect—your influence extends beyond you and touches everyone you encounter. And this influence is not fleeting. It's lasting because it is grounded in trust, integrity, and the understanding that leadership is not about the leader themselves but about the people they serve.

As you reflect on your own leadership journey, ask yourself: How can you show up more authentically? How can you use your influence, even in small ways, to create a positive impact in the lives of those around you? Authentic leadership may be quiet, but it is always powerful.

---

o o o

Chapter 12:

The Ripple Effect of Ownership

❝Ownership isn't just about accountability; it's about taking responsibility for the outcomes of your actions, and inspiring others to do the same.❞

Ownership is a powerful force in both personal and organizational growth. When you take ownership of something, whether it's a project, a relationship, or even a mistake, you claim responsibility for it. It's an acknowledgment that you have the ability to influence outcomes, and you are willing to stand by the results. Ownership is more than just a mindset; it's a way of taking proactive steps, making decisions, and committing to actions with full awareness of their impact.

At its core, ownership is about accountability. It's the understanding that the choices you make, the actions you take, and the decisions you make matter. When you take ownership, you stop blaming external factors or pointing fingers at others. You accept responsibility for your part in the situation and take action to drive change. Ownership is empowering because it allows you to shape your circumstances and take control of your outcomes.

But ownership doesn't stop at individual actions—it extends to how you influence those around you. When you demonstrate ownership, you set a standard for others to follow. Your commitment to seeing things through, taking responsibility, and delivering results inspires others to do the same. It creates a ripple effect, where your actions influence others to take ownership of their own work and lives. In turn, this creates a culture where accountability and responsibility are valued, and everyone is empowered to take charge of their actions.

When leaders embrace ownership, they create a culture of trust and transparency. A leader who takes ownership of their decisions, actions, and mistakes builds credibility and respect within their team. They model the behaviour they expect from others, setting a high standard for accountability and personal responsibility. This culture of ownership encourages everyone in the organization to act with integrity and to take full responsibility for their roles.

The ripple effect of ownership goes beyond the workplace. When individuals take ownership of their lives, their growth, and their success, they create a sense of empowerment that extends to their families, communities, and beyond. Ownership breeds confidence because it fosters a deep belief in one's ability to shape their future. It transforms individuals from passive observers of their circumstances into active creators of their reality.

This ripple effect is especially powerful in teams. When ownership becomes embedded in the culture of a group, it shifts the focus from individual tasks to collective success. People stop waiting for instructions or passing the blame; instead, they take initiative and collaborate to solve problems and create results. This sense of shared responsibility fuels innovation increases motivation and strengthens relationships within teams.

However, the ripple effect of ownership can also be seen in the way it transforms leadership itself. When leaders take ownership of their decisions and outcomes, they create a safe environment where others feel empowered to do the same. This level of transparency fosters trust and creates a deeper connection between leaders and their teams. When employees see their leader's taking ownership, they are more likely to follow suit and take ownership of their own work, leading to a more cohesive and productive team.

There is also a level of vulnerability that comes with ownership. Taking ownership means being honest about your mistakes and learning from them. It requires humility to admit when things go wrong and the strength to learn from those experiences. This vulnerability not only builds trust but also encourages others to embrace a growth mindset—understanding that mistakes are part of the journey, not a failure.

The ripple effect of ownership is not just about the direct impact of actions, but the lasting change it creates in mindsets and behaviours. It fosters a culture where individuals feel empowered to make decisions, take responsibility, and lead by example. As people take ownership, they develop a greater sense of pride in their work and a stronger commitment to delivering results. This mindset becomes ingrained, creating an environment where accountability is the norm, and everyone works together to achieve shared goals.

Ownership also challenges complacency. It forces individuals to reflect on their own contributions and the impact of their actions. Ownership makes you ask yourself: "What am I doing to contribute to the greater purpose? How am I driving results and creating value?" This constant reflection pushes individuals to take their work seriously and to strive for continuous improvement.

To truly harness the power of ownership, it requires practice and consistency. It's not enough to simply take ownership once in a while. Ownership needs to be woven into the fabric of who you are. It's a mindset that must be embraced daily, in every action, decision, and interaction. By making ownership a core value, you can create a culture of accountability, responsibility, and empowerment that extends beyond your own actions and ripples outward to influence everyone around you.

The ripple effect of ownership creates lasting change. It's the catalyst that turns individual actions into collective progress, creating a strong foundation for growth, trust, and success. When ownership is embraced, it transforms both individuals and organizations, leading to an environment where everyone feels empowered to take responsibility for their actions and make a positive impact.

As you reflect on ownership in your own life, consider: What can you take ownership of today? How can you inspire those around you to embrace ownership and make their own ripple effect in the world? When you take ownership of your actions and decisions, you not only change your life—you change the world around you.

○ ○ ○

Chapter 13:

The Legacy of Actions

"**The legacy we leave is not measured by the titles we hold, but by the lives we touch and the impact we have on others.**"

Every action you take today is a step towards the future you want to create. The choices you make, the words you speak, and the effort you put into your work all contribute to the legacy you will leave behind. A legacy is more than just the accomplishments you list on a resume or the goals you achieve in your career. It's the lasting impact you have on others and the world around you, whether immediate or far-reaching.

The truth about legacy is simple: it's built every day. Legacy isn't something you suddenly leave behind at the end of your career or life—it is the product of each decision, each conversation, and each effort you invest. As you move forward in life and leadership, it's important to realize that every action has a ripple effect. The way you lead, the way you treat people, the way you show up in the world, all become part of your legacy.

Legacy begins with intention. It's not enough to simply go through the motions or to let life pass by without reflecting on the kind of impact you want to have. To build a meaningful legacy, you must be intentional in your actions. You must ask yourself: How do I want to be remembered? What kind of difference do I want to make? What will people say about me long after I've moved on?

When you act with purpose and integrity, your actions speak louder than words. The integrity with which you live your life becomes the foundation of your legacy. It's about being consistent in your values, even when no one is watching. Your character, shaped by your actions over time, will leave a lasting imprint that transcends individual accomplishments.

Legacy is not something you leave behind when you're gone; it's something that lives on in the lives of others. Think about the people who have influenced your life. It's likely that their actions shaped the way you think, act, and lead today. This is the power of legacy. It extends beyond you to affect everyone you encounter, creating an ongoing cycle of impact that grows exponentially.

Leaders, especially, have a unique opportunity to shape the legacies of those they lead. A leader's legacy is measured not just by their own achievements, but by the successes of the people they have empowered. A true leader creates more leaders. They teach others how to think critically, act decisively, and lead with empathy and integrity. They pass on wisdom and knowledge, helping to elevate the next generation of leaders who will carry the torch forward.

Legacy also involves building something that endures. It's not about short-term gains or fleeting success. True legacy is about creating systems, processes, and cultures that stand the test of time. It's about laying down a foundation for future growth, one that continues to serve others even when you are no longer directly involved. Whether it's building a business, mentoring a team, or contributing to a cause, the impact of your actions lives on through the systems you create.

But legacy isn't only about grand gestures. It's often the small, seemingly insignificant actions that leave the most lasting impact. A kind word, a moment of encouragement, a decision made with integrity—it's in these quiet moments that legacies are truly formed. These actions, when repeated over time, weave a story that defines who you are and what you stand for.

As you look ahead, consider how you are living your legacy today. Are you being intentional in the way you act, lead, and serve others? Are you living by the values you want to pass on? Every moment is an opportunity to shape your legacy. Every choice you make, every action you take, is an investment in the legacy that will live on long after you're gone.

Legacy is not reserved for the famous or the wealthy; it is available to anyone who chooses to live a life of purpose. It's not about what you have, but what you give—your time, your talents, your knowledge, and your love. The legacy you create is defined by your actions and how you choose to make a difference in the lives of others.

In the end, your legacy is a reflection of the way you lived. It's a testament to the impact you had on others and the world around you. And while you may not be able to control how others perceive you, you can control the way you show up in the world each day. The legacy you leave is yours to define. It begins with your actions today, and it will be remembered by those who are touched by your life long after you're gone.

o o o

Chapter 14:

The Power of Priorities

"The secret to success is not in doing everything; it's in doing what matters most."

In the rush of daily life, with endless tasks and demands competing for our attention, it's easy to lose sight of what truly matters. We often find ourselves overwhelmed by the sheer volume of things we need to do, and the more we try to juggle, the less we seem to accomplish. The key to cutting through this noise and finding lasting success lies in a simple, yet powerful concept: prioritization.

Priorities are the compass that guide us toward our goals and values. They are the markers that help us distinguish between what is essential and what is simply urgent. The problem lies not in having too many things to do, but in not having a clear understanding of what should be done first, second, and what can be set aside.

Prioritizatlon is the art of making choices. It's about recognizing that time and energy are finite resources, and we cannot afford to waste them on tasks that don't align with our most important goals. This ability to focus on what matters most, while letting go of distractions, is what separates those who succeed from those who simply stay busy.

The power of prioritizing starts with self-awareness. It begins with understanding your values, your goals, and your vision for the future. Without this clarity, it's impossible to effectively prioritize because everything will feel important, and nothing will stand out. *To gain clarity, you must first pause, reflect, and ask yourself: What do I want to achieve? What are my long-term aspirations? What does success look like for me?*

Once you've identified what truly matters, the next step is aligning your daily actions with those priorities. This requires discipline and intentionality. You must be willing to say "no" to the distractions that might seem appealing in the moment, but ultimately pull you away from your purpose. It means being able to say "yes" to the hard work, the challenges, and the opportunities that will bring you closer to your goals.

This process requires reflection and regular re-evaluation. What mattered to you a year ago may no longer hold the same weight today. Life is dynamic, and so too should be your priorities. As you evolve, so too should the way you allocate your time and resources. This adaptability is crucial for long-term success because it keeps you agile, focused, and ready for the challenges that come your way.

When you prioritize effectively, you also learn to manage your energy more efficiently. It's not just about managing your time, but about ensuring that your energy is directed toward the right tasks. This means recognizing when you're at your best and aligning your most demanding tasks with your peak energy levels. It also means giving yourself permission to rest when needed, so you can return to your work with a renewed sense of focus and purpose.

Effective prioritization also involves saying no—not just to tasks, but to opportunities that do not align with your core values or long-term goals. This can be difficult, especially when faced with tempting offers or the pressure to meet external expectations. But the power to say no is a critical skill that allows you to guard your time and energy. It's a conscious choice to preserve your focus and protect your path forward.

There is also a beauty in simplification. When you focus only on what matters most, you remove the clutter and distractions that typically cloud your judgment. You streamline your efforts, making each action more impactful and purposeful. This leads to greater fulfilment, as you begin to see that your efforts are not scattered, but aligned with your true purpose.

The impact of prioritization extends beyond your personal life—it has a ripple effect in the lives of others. When you prioritize effectively, you set a powerful example for those around you. Whether you're leading a team, guiding a family, or influencing your community, the way you prioritize your time, energy, and resources speaks volumes. It inspires others to follow suit and encourages a culture of intentionality, focus, and progress.

In leadership, prioritization becomes even more critical. As a leader, you are responsible for guiding others toward shared goals, and your ability to prioritize determines how effectively you can lead. When you prioritize wisely, you can allocate resources, make decisions, and set strategies that will move your team forward. Your ability to stay focused on the big picture, while managing the details, is what keeps everyone aligned and moving in the right direction.

Ultimately, the power of priorities lies in its ability to help you live with intention and purpose. It allows you to cut through the noise and focus on what truly moves the needle in your life and career. It's about creating space for the things that matter and letting go of the rest. When you master the art of prioritization, you don't just become more productive—you become more fulfilled, because you are living in alignment with what truly matters.

As you move forward, remember that your priorities are your greatest asset. They are the map that will guide you through life's challenges, opportunities, and transitions. They are the foundation upon which you build your success, your happiness, and your legacy.

O O O

Chapter 15:

Knowing the Unknowns

> **"** *The greatest journeys are not those where we discover new lands, but where we discover new depths within ourselves.* **"**

As this book draws to a close, you may find yourself reflecting on all that has been shared, the lessons, the questions, and the introspections. But before we part ways, let's pause to embrace the essence of this journey: the unknowns.

Life is filled with uncertainties, yet it is within these uncertainties that we find our most profound opportunities. What lies ahead often feels shrouded, unclear. But it's not about having all the answers; it's about having the courage to explore, to ask, and to learn.

Through this book, we've delved into values like empathy, self-responsibility, priorities, and ownership. These aren't just concepts—they are tools for navigating the unknown. Each chapter has been a step toward discovering not just external truths but also the truths that lie within.

The Value of Values

It's tempting to see values as abstract ideas, but they are the compass that guides us in moments of doubt. They help us stand firm when the ground beneath feels shaky. Gratitude, for instance, shifts our focus from what we lack to what we have. It allows us to recognize the strength we've built and the relationships that sustain us.

As you move forward, carry these values with you—not as rigid rules but as guiding principles. Let them inspire your decisions, shape your actions, and transform your outlook.

At the heart of all exploration lies gratitude. Gratitude for the lessons learned, for the people who've shared the journey, and for the resilience that has carried you through. Be thankful not just for your successes but also for the challenges, for they've shaped the person you are today.

Owning the Path Forward

The unknowns will always exist, but they don't have to be feared. Instead, let them be invitations to grow, to adapt, and to innovate. Ownership is about more than responsibility; it's about embracing the unknown with confidence, knowing that the tools you've gathered along the way are enough.

This book is not an answer key. It's a conversation—a spark to ignite your own reflections and realizations. As you close these pages, remember that the journey doesn't end here. It begins anew with every choice you make, every path you explore, and every unknown you encounter.

> *"What you discover about yourself in the unknown will always be your greatest treasure."*

ooo